T0368290

a Handful Of Simple Poetry from Me To You

About Life's Unknowns

DAVID PETER WEIDOW

a Handful Of Simple Poetry from Me To You
About Life's Unknowns

iUniverse books may be ordered through booksellers or by contacting:

iUniverse
1663 Liberty Drive
Bloomington, IN 47403
www.iuniverse.com
844-349-9409

ISBN: 978-1-6632-0668-8 (sc)
978-1-6632-0687-9 (e)

Library of Congress Control Number: 2020914788

Print information available on the last page.

iUniverse rev. date: 09/04/2020

a Handful Of Simple Poetry from Me To You

About Life's Unknowns

Hey. Hi! I just wanted to write something about life, and the path we take doing life. I dedicate this poetry book totally to my close family, Courtney Erin Weidow, my blessing of a daughter who is my biggest fan, I might add.

Little does she know, I think her poetry and artwork are better than my own. She's great.

See, I am an artist (canvass painter), song writer, poetry writer. I am the song writer David Peter Weidow who wrote "The Devil In Me" - Majestic Records gave me a contract. Also I am the poetry writer who wrote "The Same Sun". Treasured poems of America, put a poem I wrote in their 1993 edition.

I also have Artwork paintings here and there in my book. Art work on canvass or oil. My daughter Courtney Erin Weidow will also have a poem she wrote and digital artwork found in the end of the book.

Deborah Rene Weidow. I also dedicate my poetry book to my daughter's mother and my best friend. For always being there and for cleaning up all of my messes "loose ends" as I call them.

When you read my poetry. I want you to be able to feel the words of my poetry. They come from real day to day life. "Everyday Life"

I hope you enjoy the words.

Eastern Newt

By Courtney Erin Weidow

Could life be any brighter for this tiny ambler?
Glistening slickness after a rain storm
A magical and wondrous form
Orange like the sun, sun spots included
Eyes of crushed gold, energy exuding
Wandering boldly, as if nothing can harm
Should anyone attempt – watch out, she's armed!
Did you think her color was just for show?
"Don't eat me, I'm poison, you know!"

THIS IS BECAUSE

I hold you, in my mind
The way I do
When I do
When you are here
I look
I feel
You
Anyway I want to
Yes, no
I still go
This is because
What I do
Is because me
I really love you!!!

by
Dave Weidow

HOLD ME AS I YOU

I feel with my mind
I see with my heart
What I want is you
And a brand new start
Looking at you
Is all I want to do
Take control
Can't you tell
I need you
Opening my arms
Is not just to hold you
It is to feel you
These words I say
Are so, so true
Open your arms
Hold me as I you!!!

by
Dave Weidow

I'VE SEEN THEM COME

Many dreams
I've seen come and go
When I think of it
What do I know
I've seen them come
I've seen them go
After all, what do I know
I give my mind
A little walk, a little walk
My dreams
Where'd they go, where'd they go

Who is to know
All of this, any of this
What am I to do
My jobs in life
They've just all been sliced
Some where within
Theres got to be something extra
Some where within
How have I lost so many times
Where does it all end, where does it end
I've seen them come
I've seen them go!!

by
Dave Weidow

WITH OUR EYES

When I think of you
I feel so blue
Never knowing where to go
Or what to do
I want your problems
I need all of you
We talk
Hold each other
Make love with our eyes
There is never a desire
If you are not here by my side
I always want you near
Just to have this need for you
Why all of a sudden these dreams
Because without you there are no dreams
Putting you in my world
It's from my heart, my soul
When I think of you
I feel so true!!

by
Dave Weidow

YOUR WAY

The morning light
The look deep in your eyes
Your beauty
In every way you move
Touches my heart
To the skies
Your caring ways
Enhance my feelings
That once were none
Your kindness
Gives me
All I need of you
In every way shape and form
With all your love
Inside I feel reborn
Your trail of sadness
From everytime you leave
The trace of emptyness
What I'm trying to say
Is thank you
For your touch
Your way!!

by
Dave Weidow

GIVE ME ALL YOUR LOVE

Take me, take me baby
Don't ever let me go
Give me all your love-en
Never let, never let me go
Tell me that you love me
Tell me that it's so
Hold me, hold me so gently
As you once used to do
Never forget who I am
Or how far we have come
Take me, take me baby
Say that it's true girl
I'm the only one for you
Blue skies
And sometimes dirt flies
Life just wouldn't be the same
Without you
Without you, can't you see
Give me all your love-en
Give me all your love!!

by
Dave Weidow

TO SEE WHO I AM

I don't know what to say
I don't know what to do
What ever I try
It's so hard for me
Give me a chance
Let my life dance
Don't let me down
I know it seems
I'm never around
But what can I do
There is more to life
Than me and you
It might look to be untrue
I am what I am
Not much in other eyes
What you see is me
No matter what
I want to be

Life can be so fun
It will run and run and run
You know how I've tried
No matter what
You are my love
Don't take that from me
Open your world
To see what it's like
Open your mind
To see who I am
Don't give a damn
Take the chance
Give what you are
Make another try
Make your life dance!!!

by
Dave Weidow

BACK IN MY SOUL

I called, you were there
My first thought
All my memories
I wanted to share
My love you didn't know
Yet so strong it was
Talking to your voice
Gave me no choice
I wanted it as it was
Before, so alive
To think the way it is
The way it will be
Again with all my might
This feeling stunned me
It was like it never ended
I had to make myself know
I imagined you in my arms
Back in my world
Back in my soul!!

by
Dave Weidow

BE REAL

Open with some words
To say just how I feel
For all the crazy things I wanted
I've been so sorry I haven't made them real
I try and try to please you
You say I already do
What is it in this world
I can't make them happen
The way I want to
Yes, I do love you
With everything I have, it's true
I've been feeling kind of strange inside
It's all because of you
In every way I don't mean to hurt you
And it seems in every way I do
Say the words you really feel
Help me, help me be real!!

by
Dave Weidow

ALLS I WANT

Sometimes I see your face
In my mind and your not here
The things I've done
Hurt me so
And I want to hold you
And your not near
What I've done
Is in my memory
It will be, forever and ever
My love for you
Is so true
I can't believe
The things someone like me could do
I've wanted you for all my life
What has happened
Can not be me and you
Alls I want is to give you
Alls I want is to have you
Alls I want is you!!

by
Dave Weidow

I REALLY REACH

Your eyes of brown
Your heart of blue
Are memories of gold
That I once knew
Bodies of steel
Still looking back
Yesterday is real
Others who have passed
Others so close
And you hold so dear
The days have been going by
The days have went and gone
Looking around the days are so sound
But nothing has changed
Look, the glass, it's the same all around
Only the pictures have changed
I reach, I really reach
The glass
The pictures
Once I used to know
I reach
I really reach!!

by
Dave Weidow

SPARKS THAT FLY

You might think
You are not my rose
But my love
Oh how it grows
You give me life
Beneath the soul
You give me love
And I need it so
Hold me so tight
Hold me
Don't let me know
Just how much
You really love me so

Make me learn
Of what you are
To find the ways
Beneath the scars
Your hopes
Make me grow and grow
Your beauty itself
Makes me see
Sparks that fly
For only you and me
Sparks that fly!!!

by
Dave Weidow

YOU MUST KNOW

Morning sunset
Awaits the new day
Ever lasting deepness
Wondering, is there a way
Open so many new feelings
Sometimes finding no words to say
Uneasy the person inside
No one knows the path he was betrayed
Living in a shadow
He walks a fine line
Where always, a dead end
Giving what seems to be enough
Looking around for something more
The thrill of living is at a stand still
I need some place to give my all
I have tried so, so many times
Still to find nothing more
Than what was at the start
Finding yourself a real dream
Morning sunset
You must know has passed!!

by
Dave Weidow

WHAT AM I TO DO

Yesterday I used to say
It was a dream
As far as I'm concerned
Now the time
It is so near
What am I to do
All my hopes
I once talked about
Are faded in the wind
All my hopes
Are almost gone
Now I know what it feels like
What it really feels like
Now to be in those shoes
What am I to do
Your brown eyes look so true
Now you see me in those shoes
What am I to do!!

by
Dave Weidow

MY OTHER FACE

POEM

What to expect

When I myself

Can't figure out things that I have done

The very reason I lose my mind

Is because theres no one

Who cares enough to stop me

Maybe I do know it's my own foolishness

I want nothing, but I want everything

The world around me is always wrong

When truely it's always been me

I seem to never face the facts

About the real person I am

I always want more
And never change what faces I have
There is just one big explosion
Going on in my mind, and around me
Which myself causes it all
Yet I want it stopped
And keep fooling myself over and over
Sometimes I wonder if I really
Want this all changed
The only one who would know this
Would be my other face
That I hide underneath the true me!!!

by
Dave Weidow

THEY ONCE KNEW

No one listens to what
I say anymore
I don't even really think
They care about me
Sometimes before
They use to sit back
With pain in their eyes
They once knew the hard times
I was going through
Now it seems it's all brand new
Life has changed
And I think they have to
Theres nothing left for me to do!!

by
Dave Weidow

GIVEN HEARTS

Certain people
Seem to fail
Only wise
To the way we hail
Tightened friendships
Turning stale
Glossy memories
Visions turning pale
Lively feelings
Frightened to fight
To stay alive
Given hearts

To those who take
For only I
Lose the choice
Because of my mistakes
Turning pages
Come alive
Fight to save memories
For I strive to see the true
Given hearts
To seek it through
Taking yours for what is now
Time has stumbled
For times have changed
And where are you!!

by
Dave Weidow

CREATED

What is there to happen
When the open heart
Becomes of strain
Time is never a substance
The nights no matter how warm and filled
Seem to be cold and empty
Alone as you sit wondering
Can't help to think
You've seen what can happen
To every breath you have taken
The changes that are so sudden
Creep up among the sturdy
Fear a point to be the issue
Is created by the thought
Secure in the mind
To make your lifes cast so much easier
You bother to go out of your way
To feel privileged enough to care
Your thoughts never stop to deceive
Distance of many light years
You have traveled
Makes the core your own little world!!!

CAN'T BE THE SAME

Railroad tracks and wooden boards
That's how I'll find my home
Flowing the hardened ground
Covering up from the storm
Taking every slow step
Trying to live my own ways
Life seems to be so hard
I can't find what I'm looking for
The life I'm living can't be the same
That's why I take my chances
I don't need anyone elses blame
Living my life from the earth
See the view over looking the field

Trying not to miss my birth place
Home on the farm
Giving up what I had
Trying to see this is my world
What can a man like me find
When he doesn't no where to go
Or what I'm looking for
It can't only be me
That walks his every way
Given time I'll find a home
A place to lay my hat
Taking my chances!!

by
Dave Weidow

That keeps me living
But yet holds me back from my world
True to you my mind is not open at all
Where do all my stories come from
What page can I turn to, to live my own life!!!

by
Dave Weidow

WHAT HAS HAPPENED

Up in the attic
Things put away
Yesterdays dreams
Make you what you are today
Times you were lonely
Memories just put away
The past I almost forgot
Todays world not the same
People changing
We aren't the blame
One different move
One different flame
Takes the heart far away
Wise choices
Make your name
Given rights
To a certain fame!!!

by
Dave Weidow

ROOM

My room is cozy
The heat
Just warm
My feelings
Involved
My hope
Just standing still
Everything is okay
But not good enough
The past is gone
But yet
I am here
My world
The same
Time
Just passing!!!

by
Dave Weidow

MEMORIES LOST OVER TIME

Mystery has no part

Learn, begin a new start

Time forbids you

Phases of reality

Memories lost over time

Given love

Speak for only yourself

Love others as you wish to be loved

Kindly give

Whatever it takes

To be given

Lust for a new start

Make your beginning

For what you feel

Theres only one you

You must keep together

Not be apart

Fight together for what is yours

Time is real!!!

by
Dave Weidow

WHERE AM I GOING

I'm on a road
Along way from home
Mixed emotions
I'm all alone
I have lovers
I have no love
Things I see
Pictures I can't follow
Stories that don't match
Life in the gutter
Minds on each other
No one to care

Good people all gone
Time just changing
Different numbers
New life to ruin
Fresh love to waste
Hearts to break
Good persons so different
Living in a world
That just can't be beat
Where am I going
What skies are blue
Where is the road
Yes I am different than you!!!

by

Dave Weidow

NO ANSWER

For my life
I feel
There is no tomorrow
I have nothing
What is there
There is nothing
I love what I want to be
No matter what I'm trying to say
There is no one else
That could ever see
My feelings are real
I know there is more to life
There has got to be
My feelings
On the way I try
Are limited
Know matter what I say
Things may never change
Though I hurt
It doesen't matter
For I have hurt many
There is no longer feelings
No one really cares
About anything
So why must I!!

OR THOUGH IT SEEMS

Many times I sit alone
Wondering what has been so bad
What have I done
That makes me feel so wrong all the time
Many times I've done so right
Seems like I forget
Like it's over night
Sitting here now
I see life could be better to me
If I was only better to life
Why, why do I ask myself these questions
When no one else does
Or even bothers to ask or notice
Whats a world made of
If people stop wondering why
Or don't bother to ask
There are many questions
Where am I to begin
What is there that is more important than life
I guess it's how I live it
Or though it seems!!!

by
Dave Weidow

WHAT I LOVE

I love my life
I really love
All I see
The life I've had
From what I live
And see
Would not be so bad
If it were not for me
My life I live
For all there is
I'd give it all
Just for happiness
I have done many things
To be ashamed
Many times
I could have done more
The answers I've come up with
I know could have been more sure
I know I could have had more!!

by
Dave Weidow

IT MIGHT BE YOU

You know him
You think you do
You don't
But you want to
Many times
You try to
Many times
You wanted to
Never change
Because it hurts you
Look around
It might be you!!

by
Dave Weidow

HOPES

For love is your shadow
Time is your, you
Give yourself chances
Lifes dreams will come true!!

by
Dave Weidow

THE DARK ME

I really do love

The world I'm in

If people listen

I would speak

I'm not afraid

I'm just me

I do many wrongs

If theres such a thing

As rights

I really do know

Deep down

In the dark of me

What I'm all about

By my mistakes, I will learn

The deepest part of me!!!

by

Dave Weidow

SOMEDAY

Hardened a man I am
Who am I
Why am I
See me with pain
See me
I'm insane
Where to go
What to do
The man that I am
Why I am untrue
I don't know
Love me
Don't turn me blue
What am I
No one, is it true?
Bad things I've done, maybe
But I've been trying lately
Someday your right
Someday!!!
I'll see

by
Dave Weidow

In My World

My mind is burning
For words to say
My feelings are open
Because I want to share them that way
In my heart
Of the brick wall I've shattered, that stands before me
My thoughts are vigorously trembling
In my mind
I know what stands before me
In my soul
I've lived it
In my world
I have built it!!

by
Dave Weidow

IF I ONLY KNEW

I live this life
For there is nothing more
Trapped on earth
I must fight to score
There is no hurt or feeling anymore
All there is, is to settle the score
I have no time to fight the wrong
For what comes tomorrow
I may not be that strong
From what false lies
Should I seek true
For who to believe
If I only knew!

by
Dave Weidow

TO SUCCEED

When you need someone, you know
Or sometimes just anyone
Around to care for you
And your feeling lonely
You just need someone to hold you
And theres no one there
You can look every where
And the room could be so filled
Yet your so alone, so empty
You try to be happy
And to others you are

But you know
They just don't see
The inside that's you
They just don't realize the loss
You have taken in your life
But you don't let that stop you
Many things you make happen in your world
To bring you to the point
That tomorrow is unspoken for
Fresh like starting over
The only thing you have to remember
Is that there is nothing to stop you
Take stride, your you
Make your own path to succeed!!!!!

by

Dave Weidow

IN A WORLD OF MY OWN

My life

Is just living

Tears keep me sane

I'm in a world of my own

I am hurt but not shattered

The existing

Is not a man

Learn

Seek forbidden

Encounters

Take note

For the scare

Gets longer

Your wall

Gets thicker

Yet tears

Still yet

Tears cloud your view!!!

by

Dave Weidow

JUST FOR TOMORROW

I'm sitting here
With a flame
Of bright memories
I'm living
Just for tomorrow
What I will find
I can only imagine
In my deepest day dreams
I hear my heart thumping
I feel a most loss
Discomfort
That only a lonely person
Could ever feel
I have nothing
That I really want
Just needs
And as I pray here
I'd give my life
For a world
I could live in
As I lay here
My heart turns pure
And my goal comes forth!!!

by
Dave Weidow

AM I IN

When I'm in a stage
Of no control
I find it hard
Not to speak the truth
I find it hard
To be retained
I open
Feed my need
I lost
My respect fell to my knees
In my head
There were no straight lines
In my body
There was no stopping me
My friends
Were subjects
I need more
To be more
I've got to get out
Of being lost!!!

by
Dave Weidow

MEND MY WAYS

I will mend my ways
A million times
I will give
Everything
Even what I am
I try so dearly
I try just to stay alive
My strength can't hold
A lust of many door ways
The opening
Of my old life
To my new life

I can't make bad times
To the living dreams
Of what I need to have
My mind is frightened
Of what I know
Because lifes so simple
And the people make it
A dream, just a dream
Who will
Try your strength
Of lust
Of many door ways!!!

by
Dave Weidow

THE END

I try so hard
Just to live my life
I try giving love
To those who care
Sometimes you get stepped on
By friends
Who really are not
Sometimes your love
Is forgotten
Theres people you meet
That give themselves
To anyone

There are those
Who really care
You love someone
They love you back
You fall in love
Then your feelings change
You tell them you don't
Love them
They hurt, they cry
And leave with someone else
Even if it isn't really over
It's the end!!!

by
Dave Weidow

MY LIFE THE SAME

The trees
It's winter
The cold
Seems forever
The snow
Is falling
The ground
So hard
My life
The same
The wind
Pushes onward

The sky
So bold
My life
The same
Just keep
Going on
Memories
Always flashing
Time
To slow
To tell
My life
The same!!

by
Dave Weidow

OF WHAT

Wind blowing
Faces hide
Minds wondering
No control
Life goes on
The wind
Still blows
Faces still hide
Minds still wondering
Of no control
Time gives in
Little of
We know
It happens
Right before us
There is no stopping
The mind
Of within
We ask ourselves
Can't we see
The answer is
Of what!!!

by
Dave Weidow

THE TRUE

True to myself
Only within
Mounted
Between a hardened wall
With much sin
Nothing to live for
No one to hold
Grasp your lover
Try for softness
Not to be so bold!!!

by
Dave Weidow

ALL ALONE

The little time
I spend all alone
I have thought
Of many memories
I see what is
I feel what isn't
I'm afraid
Of being not
Afraid
I try hard in life
To mend my ways
I give hope
I give nothing
Try understanding
For what is
Don't waste
What isn't
Give what there is
Not for truth
Of what could be
Think and learn
Tremble
With no fear!!!

by
Dave Weidow

Skin

I was walking, one foot in front of the other
In my pathway, it zigzaged
I was following with my head down
This S-shaped pathway
My skin began to crawl
As I slithered across the desert sand
The sandstorm wiped away my pathway
When I turned around to look, the snake became part of me

Benzo

I took another pill, minus one from one twenty
The yellow stain was on my tongue
I began to not feel anything
As through time, I heal
But the Percocet prescription don't seem real
As I empty the last of the bottle in my hand, I
realize it's only 16 days later
From a prescription that was written for 30 days
I shake the bottle, I hold it to the light
To my amazement, I realize what I have done
The pain is pounding in my head
As I could have sworn, it was in my back

Ass

I got out of bed in the morning like always
Took my shower, dragging my head
She told me she could never get that far
This was a week later
And she said she smelled like ass
Depression set in for many days
Finally, once she got her shower, her day got better
The morning after, she remembered the day before
And she got up and out of bed, and did it all again

The Fire

The crackling of smoke
Hickory
Becomes the flame
As I sit on the flagstone, I feel the heat within me
I reach out with one hand
I am like a butterfly
I feel the need with my antennae sticking out
I realize I am in deep thought
As I add another piece of hickory to the fire, I realize how cold I am within
Wishing for a fireplace that does not exist

Simple

I am slippery like a snake
I feel the vibration from the ground
As I slither my S-shaped body all around
I am inside, I am outside
I conquer the world as I see it, as I feel it
And you tell me I don't have a backbone?

Outside

I sit here knowing I have loved from way beyond a mile

I am loved much higher than the clouds in the sky

As I move them, I see the ones I love with my eye

Strong, with strength behind the clouds, you will never see me cry

I am within myself as many

Outside, you don't even see me

I don't try to hide my darkness, as I burst with power from within

You know who I am, Father figure and all

Thinking of your future, that is me

You know what I'm talking about – you see –

You definitely are my little girl

Power down to no one

I may step in shit, but no rose I smell like

Within

Outside, I am

still

Herbal Tea

Finally, I found a clean cup
I was out of mud, so I filled it with hot tea
The herbs and spices that I smelled, made my nerves tingle in my body
My awareness became tenfold
All I could remember, are the years that went by, and I feel so old
Again, I found a clean cup, and forgetting about my age
Forget the mud
The herbs and spices of the tea
Unbelievably became part of me

Fresh Smell

I walked in the door of the kitchen

The garbage lid was up

It smelled from last night's gravy from supper

I went into the bathroom next to the kitchen

The trash lid smelled, so I washed it

My hands came next because of the germs from the lid

I had to change the bag in the trash can

It ripped as I tried to remove it

I took the garbage down to where the garbage man was coming

Beforehand, I put a new bag in the garbage can

I waved to the garbage man as he went

I came back up to the kitchen, sat down in my chair at the table

I resumed painting what I was painting

That awful smell finally went away

As my painting grew into a rose

The fresh smell was all that was in the air

Dinosaur

The rumble of the Earth reminded me of yester years
The vibration went through my whole body
As I looked up, as the shadow
I realized it was not me
The rumble shook me
As the look on the dinosaur's face became a smile because he saved me

An Air

I dream of the air
that you can see
right through
and you breathe
and feel the nice flow
going down your throat
And than a dusty wind blows
and you go place to place
and see everything.
No matter what it is
you see it
you're free
as free as can be
You're on your own
all by yourself,
just blowing by.
I dream of the clouds
that I must go by
and must see
close.
And go through,
and moving them across
the sky,

the power I have
and all I am is a big area of air
what a feeling.
And last night I dreamed of myself
like the king of the world,
no one or nothing is like I am
And the feeling I have
makes it worthwhile
to be what I am.
But it's great
And very lonely
when you are all alone
But you're all by yourself
and you have all that time
to see and think
whatever you want
Ain't it great
to think whatever
you want to
or say whatever you want to?
No one will
or can stop you
It's just to great
and they know it
(and they feel it)

I'm different from you because
I have all the time
and space in the world,
His all mine
No one else
can ever have the feeling
of pure good flowing air
and the freedom that I have
and if they could
I guess I wouldn't
have the feeling I do
if everyone had it
We both are the same
In one way -
We have air at some time
but wouldn't it be great
to be air
to feel the freeness of life
as I see it.
It's more than I can handle myself
That's why it's so great

David Peter Weidow

Photography

Done By

Courtney Erin Weidow

Eastern Newt

by Courtney Erin Weidow

Could life be any brighter for this tiny ambler?
Glistening slickness after a rain storm
A magical and wondrous form
Orange like the sun, sun spots included
Eyes of crushed gold, energy exuding
Wandering boldly, as if nothing can harm
Should anyone attempt–watch out, she's armed!
Did you think her color was just for show?
"Don't eat me, I'm poison, you know!"

5-23-20

I'M BACK

Hey. I wanted to end with something. So here it is. I went down many different paths in my life. I always try to make something happen to better myself with the very little time we have on earth. I always say

"LETS DO IT"
"AND DO IT RIGHT"

Thank you for your time,
David Peter Weidow

Printed in the United States
By Bookmasters